They are **stars.**

Stars are big balls of **gas.**

Stars give off light and heat.

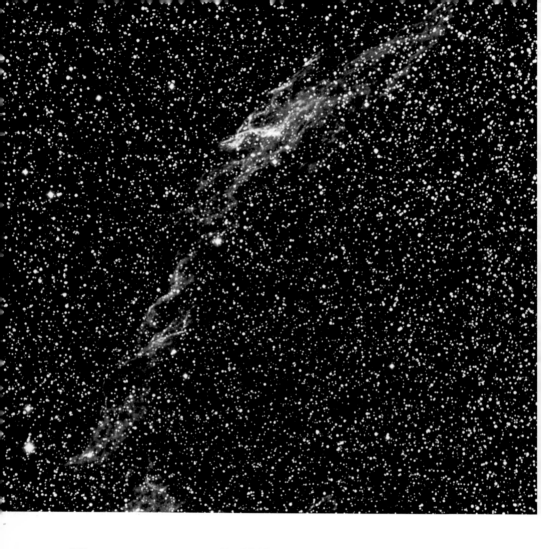

There are **trillions** of stars in space.

Stars are all different sizes.

Stars look small because
they are far away.

Most stars are bigger than Earth.

Our closest star is the Sun.

The Sun gives Earth light
and heat.

Stars do not live forever.

When a star dies, it
explodes.

People give groups of stars names.

This group is called the Big Dipper.

We can see stars better with
telescopes.

It is fun to look at stars.

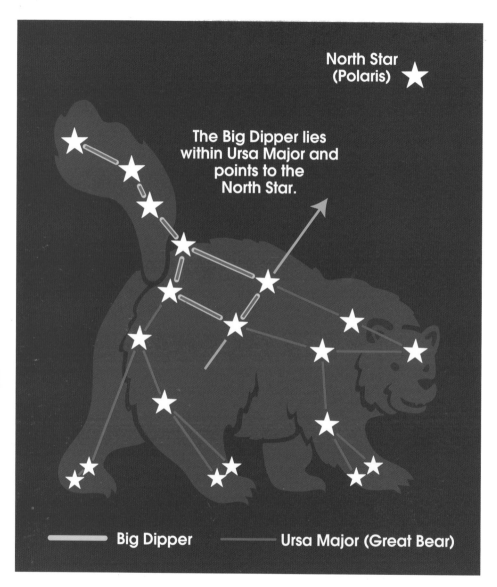

North Star (Polaris)

The Big Dipper lies within Ursa Major and points to the North Star.

Big Dipper — Ursa Major (Great Bear)

Constellations

There are many stars in the sky. Some groups of stars look like dot-to-dot pictures of animals, people, or objects. These star pictures are called constellations. They are often named for the pictures they show. One famous constellation is Ursa Major, which means Great Bear. Another is Taurus, the Bull.

Stars Fun Facts

The brightest star in the sky is called Sirius, the Dog Star. It is 51 trillion miles, or 8.7 light-years, from Earth.

Stars are not just white. They are many different colors. The coolest stars are red, and the hottest stars are blue.

The biggest stars are called Supergiants. They can be 100 times larger than the Sun.

A shooting star is not a star at all. It is really a meteor falling through space.

Most stars live to be about 10 billion years old.

Shurnarkabtishashutu is the star with the longest name. Its name means *under the southern horn of the bull.*

Glossary

 explodes – blows up with a loud noise

 gas – something that is not liquid or solid

 stars – heavenly bodies that give off light and heat

 telescopes – tools that make faraway things look closer

 trillions – more than one million millions

Index

The photographs in this book are reproduced through the courtesy of: © Roger Ressmeyer/ CORBIS, front cover; © Bert Krages/Visuals Unlimited, p. 2; © NASA, p.3; © Science VU/Visuals Unlimited, pp. 4, 15, 22 (second from top); © GoodShoot/SuperStock, p. 5; © California Institute of Technology, p. 6, 22 (bottom); © SuperStock, p. 7; © John Sanford, p. 8; © PhotoDisc Royalty Free by Getty Images, p. 9; © Arthur Morris/Visuals Unlimited, p. 10; © John Sanford/Astrostock, pp. 11, 22 (middle); © R. Hull/Astrostock, p. 12; © Subaru Telescope/Astrostock, pp. 13, 22 (top); © Mug Shots/CORBIS, p. 14;© RDF/Visuals Unlimited, pp. 16, 22 (second from bottom); © Dale O'Dell/CORBIS, p. 17.

Lerner Publications Company
A division of Lerner Publishing Group
241 First Avenue North
Minneapolis, MN 55401 USA

Website address: www.lernerbooks.com

Library of Congress Cataloging-in-Publication Data

Mitchell, Melanie S.
     Stars / by Melanie Mitchell.
         p.   cm. — (First step nonfiction)
     Includes index.
     Summary: A simple introduction to the characteristics of stars.
     ISBN: 0–8225–5138–1 (lib. bdg. : alk. paper)
     ISBN: 0–8225–3592–0 (pbk. : alk. paper)
     1. Stars—Juvenile literature. [1. Stars.] I. Title. II. Series.
QB801.7.M64 2004
523.8—dc21   2003005630

Manufactured in the United States of America
1 2 3 4 5 6 – DP – 09 08 07 06 05 04